the little book of

HOUSE PLANTS

and other greenery

emma sibley

photography by adam laycock

Hardie Grant

QUADRILLE

I would love to dedicate this book to my grandparents, Ben and Ethel Howard, for passing on their green fingers to me.

CONTENTS

---

6   INTRODUCTION

9   CHOOSING YOUR PLANTS

10   POTTING AND TOOLS

12   PROPAGATION

14   TROUBLESHOOTING

16   HOUSE PLANTS AND OTHER GREENERY

138   INDEX

141   GLOSSARY

142   SUPPLIERS

143   ABOUT THE AUTHOR

INTRODUCTION

PLANTS FOR THE HOME

———

House plants are having their time at the moment. Whether it is a small collection of potted window plants or a larger stand-alone piece, any home can benefit from the addition of house plants. Surrounding yourself with greenery is not only known to help lift your mood, inspire ideas and create a sense of calm, but plants also purify the air around you by reducing airborne dust particles and removing pollutants.

Today, there are so many house plants available, from the various patterned leaves of a *Calathea* to the pancake-leaf shape of the *Pilea* or the deeply cut-out *Monstera* — you're spoilt for choice.

With such a variety of plants available to purchase and expand your house plant family, it can be tricky to give each plant the exact care that it needs in order to thrive in your home. This book will help you nurture and care for your individual plants, explaining when and how to water, how much sun is needed and how to propagate each plant in order to grow or share your collection.

HOW TO USE THIS BOOK

Each entry includes key information about caring for that particular plant. All the information is clearly organised under appropriate symbols which will help you give your plants everything they need to grow and thrive.

KEY TO SYMBOLS

☀	LIGHT	⌀	PROPAGATION
◊	WATER	⚠	WATCH OUT FOR
⚘	GROWTH AND CARE	?	DID YOU KNOW
⊔	POTTING	≈	HUMIDITY
⊔⊔	REPOTTING	◊	TEMPERATURE
✂	PRUNING		

Each plant is given its common and Latin names; occasionally these are the same. The Latin or botanical name provides information about the relationship between plants and is known as the taxonomic status. All plants belong to a particular family and these are divided into *genera* (the plural of *genus*). The Latin name of each plant consists of two words: the *genus* and the species. The *genus* is a collective name for a group of plants, and the species (or specific epithet) tells you more about a particular plant.

CHOOSING YOUR PLANTS

When it comes to purchasing the right plant it is best to do it in person. There are a few online retailers now that can post plants straight to your door, but as convenient as this can be I think it is best to visit your local nursery, garden centre or plant shop. You will then be able to pick out what you want from the selection and chat to the people who work there to make sure you are getting the right plant for your home.

When you have chosen your plant, now is the time to check for any signs of disease (browning leaves or yellow dots) or visible pests, as you do not want a diseased plant or to risk affecting the rest of your collection.

Buying house plants can be addictive. You never seem to have enough and there is always room for one more! You will find plants that like to sit next to each other: ferns and *Calathea* can be friends because they both like high humidity so will enjoy a good misting, and *Begonias* do not like getting too much water on their leaves, so will prefer to be placed away from the ferns.

Use your hanging and trailing plants to break up your bookshelf or display them from a ceiling hook. It is always important to give each plant enough room to grow, as you don't want the aerial roots from your giant *Monstera* to start creeping into the pots of your smaller plants, others such as the Paper Plant like plenty of room to extend their long arms without obstruction. A large collection is great but make sure you have the correct space and enough light to keep everyone happy!

POTTING AND TOOLS

ESSENTIAL EQUIPMENT

CONTAINERS AND OTHER TOOLS

Most plants you bring home will come in plastic or terracotta pots.
These will need to be placed inside another decorative pot without a
hole, so the plastic pot can drain through, or you can use a plastic dish
under the original pot. It is always useful to have a trowel and a sturdy
pair of gardening gloves handy for mixing soil and repotting plants.

COMPOST

For most house plants a general potting or multipurpose compost
will be sufficient. Use organic compost if you want to avoid insecticides.

WATERING

A small watering can and mister is essential to keep humidity high
and your plants hydrated.

SNIPS

It is a good idea to get yourself a small
pair of snips. These will be very helpful
when pruning and propagating
your house plants.

ADDING HUMIDITY
TO YOUR COLLECTION

Many house plants require a high humidity in order to flourish. Unfortunately due to city life and central heating most environments in the home are very dry and you will need to alter the humidity in the surrounding environment.

MISTING

No matter how much you water a plant, it will not help with the humidity, so you will need to mist the surrounding air and leaves to increase this. However, double check specific plants as some require a high humidity but do not like water gathering on their leaves, so another method may be better for them.

PEBBLE TRAY

Grouping plants together on a pebble tray filled with water can be beneficial to plants that do not appreciate water on their leaves. The pebbles ensure that the plants do not take up excess water, which can lead to root rot, so as the water evaporates from the tray it creates a high humidity, which will get trapped between the leaves of the plants.

PROPAGATION

THE PROCESS OF CREATING
NEW PLANTS FROM A CUTTING,
AN OFFSET OR A SEED.

———

Propagation is the process of creating new plants from a cutting or by separating the plant at the repotting stage. You can also propagate plants from seed, but this is a lengthier process, so we are just going to concentrate on the first two methods.

CUTTINGS

Many plants such as *Pilea*, *Saxifraga* and Spider Plants produce pups or offshoots (small shoots of themselves), which are found from shoots or nestled into the main stem of the parent. Once they start to root, they can be cut off and placed in a new pot with some potting compost and will quickly grow to become a parent plant themselves.

Both leaf and stem cuttings can also be very successful for propagation. Simply trim the leaf or stem a few centimetres below the growing point and place in a cup of water. Within a few weeks you should be able to see a new root network growing from the bottom of the stem, which can then be planted in potting compost.

SEPARATING YOUR PLANT

Plants that are made up of lots of individual stems or clumps, such as Asparagus Ferns or *Calathea*, can easily be separated when repotting to create more plants. Repot your plants in early spring just before the main growing season, as this will give the new plantlets the best chance once separated.

Gently take the plant out of the pot and dust off as much compost as possible; this will make it easier to separate the roots without too much damage. A sharp blade can be handy here to carefully separate the plants, but as long as each section carries a healthy amount of roots and leaves they will be happy transferring to their new pots. Once in their new pot keep the soil moist until the plant is properly established.

TROUBLESHOOTING

COMMON PROBLEMS AND THEIR SOLUTIONS

———

Most house plants require different levels of sun, water and care, so beware of falling at certain hurdles.

OVERWATERING
Overwatering through the winter when most plants go into dormancy is a common error. In most instances you will need to decrease watering to once every two weeks otherwise the roots may sit in water, which can cause root rot. Other side effects of overwatering is leaves wilting and yellowing, or starting to drop off and turn brown.

SCORCHING AND BURNING
Scorching and burnt leaves can also be a problem for some house plants. Too much direct sunshine can harm delicate leaves so if you notice brown marks and crispy edges, then move your plant to another position. A lack of sun can also be a problem as it may stunt the growth of the plant or stop the plant from flowering. If this happens, move your plant to another spot.

PESTS
If the compost is too damp for your plants this can attract lots of pests, including the fungus gnat or sciarid fly. These tiny black flies deposit their larvae in the damp compost, and are mostly harmless to the plants.

The best solution is to allow the compost to dry out completely between watering or to repot the whole plant.

One way to prevent pests making their home in and around your plant is to remove any wilting leaves or dead matter that has accumulated in the pot below the plant, as this provides the perfect environment for mealy bugs and spider mites to thrive.

NO GROWTH

If you have had a plant for a while and have noticed no signs of growth, this could be caused by a number of things. It could be due to underwatering in the summer or overwatering in the winter. Another possible cause is stunted growth which can happen when you haven't repotted your plant for a long time. Plants should ideally be repotted as they grow. If a plant is not repotted its roots can become cramped and root-bound.

SHEDDING

If your plant seems to be shedding a lot of leaves this could be an indication that there has been a change in temperature or that you are underwatering. It is important to be aware that shedding is a natural process by which plants self-propagate. If you are concerned then try moving your plant to a new location.

HOUSE PLANTS

AND OTHER GREENERY

This dainty purple plant reacts to dull light or the evening drawing in by bowing the three petals on each of its stems. Throughout the summer months you will notice a scattering of white tubular flowers, which only last a few days before dying back and making way for the next round. It is a good idea to pull out any dead stems and flowers to keep your *Oxalis* looking fresh.

FALSE SHAMROCK

OXALIS TRIANGULARIS

LIGHT:

Enjoying indirect sunshine and partial shade, *Oxalis* will appreciate a bright room with plenty of natural light. Be careful not to leave it in direct sunshine though as this may burn and scar the leaves.

WATER:

Your *Oxalis* will need regular watering once a week. Keep the compost damp and make sure the pot isn't sitting in a pool of water as this can promote root rot.

PROPAGATION:

Oxalis can be easily propagated through separation. Be gentle as you ease the plant apart and carefully separate it so as not to damage the roots.

GROWTH AND CARE:

As the *Oxalis* grows quite compactly, you will rarely need to repot it. When new growth occurs it is rapid but once the plant is established or when there is no space for it to grow into, it's growth will slow down, at which point you can repot.

Just because you don't live in a tropical region where Banana Plants are plentiful doesn't mean you cannot grow one happily in your home. Be aware that a Banana Plant can become rather large, so you may want to opt for a dwarf variety as this will be much easier to care for and move around if needed.

BANANA PLANT

MUSA ORIANA

LIGHT: Unlike most house plants, the Banana Plant will actually tolerate and thrive in some direct light, so keep it in a warm, bright room. However, it will not cope well with cold draughts.

WATER: Indoor Banana Plants actually need more water than those that grow outside, but watch out for overwatering and root rot. Plenty of drainage is a must.

WATCH OUT FOR: Be careful when placing a Banana Plant in your home as the large leaves are paper-thin and can tear and break very easily.

POTTING: Given the right conditions a Banana Plant can grow big very quickly and reward you with a new leaf every week or so. Young pups need frequent repotting due to the speed in which they can grow - this could be up to 2-3 times in the first year. As your Banana Plant ages it will happily stay in the same pot for a lot longer without the need for more space.

You'll find the smaller trailing, cousin of the *Monstera deliciosa*, *Monstera obliqua* hanging from suspended baskets. Remarkably the natural oval holes in the leaves of *Monstera obliqua* appear almost as soon as the new leaf uncurls, which makes it a delicate plant to repot as you must be careful not to tear the leaves. Most of the plant you will find in a mass around the top of the pot, but there is always at least one long stem which likes to hang freely, gaining length throughout the year. It can be trained to climb a moss pole.

SWISS CHEESE VINE

MONSTERA OBLIQUA

LIGHT:

Enjoying much the same light as *Monstera deliciosa*, this plant will thrive in a bright room, as long as it is kept away from direct sunshine.

WATER:

Keep the compost damp and do not overwater or allow the pot to stand in a pool of water as this can promote root rot. Misting regularly and wiping the leaves will help remove dust and keep your *Monstera obliqua* looking fresh.

PROPAGATION:

Monstera obliqua is easy to propagate. Simply take a cutting that includes at least two leaf nodes and pop it into a cup of water. Wait for roots to appear and then repot into fresh, moist compost, watering regularly at first.

The leaves of this plant could have come straight from the Jurassic period. With its vibrant green arrow-shaped leaves lined with the faded darker green, it becomes obvious where this plant got the name 'Dragon Scale'.

DRAGON SCALE ALOCASIA 'DRAGON SCALE'

LIGHT:

Like most *Alocasia*, this plant enjoys a bright but indirect sunlight, but keep it warm and do not allow it to sit in a cold, dark corner as this will stunt the growth and cause the vibrant colour on the leaves to fade.

WATER:

Water regularly in summer, about once a week, but allow the compost to dry out slightly before re-watering. The roots of this plant are particularly susceptible to root rot so do not completely soak the compost or leave the roots in a dish of water. During winter, water less frequently, allowing the compost to almost completely dry out. Mist your plant throughout the year, as it thrives in the humidity.

PRUNING:

Remove any yellow or brown leaves, especially if you spot any black spots, as this could be a sign of fungal disease.

WATCH OUT FOR:

Alocasia can be poisonous to pets and small children so keep out of their reach.

Starting with a young **Rubber Plant** will give you the most success at home as the plant will easily adapt to the surroundings you provide it with. There are a few varieties to look out for with the rubber plant, including the variegated *Ficus elastica* 'Tricolour', *Ficus elastica* 'Triangularis' and the ever-popular *Ficus elastica* 'Black Prince' with its dark green, almost black, leathery leaves. All varieties are quite hardy and if you keep to a few basic rules you should have a tall specimen in no time.

RUBBER PLANT FICUS ELASTICA

LIGHT:

Bright but indirect light is the best conditions for *Ficus elastica*.

WATER:

During summer it is important that the compost never dries out too much, so watering once a week without waterlogging should be enough. However, during the winter dormant period, water once every two weeks, allowing the compost to dry out between watering. If during this time the leaves start to turn brown or fall off then it is an indication that you need to increase watering slightly. Regular misting and wiping of the leaves is also advised.

PROPAGATION:

The easiest method of propagation for this plant is to cut off a stem and place it in either a potting and rooting mixture, or leave in a cup of water to root before planting up.

This plant can survive attached to a host plant as long as the host is big enough to support its growth, but in the home it may be best to grow it in a pot. This plant is generally grown for its showy, bright, red and orange flower heads, which bear a small cluster of white blooms in the centre. When viewed from above it takes on the appearance of a star, hence the name.

SCARLET STAR GUZMANIA LINGULATA

LIGHT: The Scarlet Star prefers bright but indirect sunlight at all times, as depriving it of light will cause the colours to fade from both the leaves and flower. However, too much direct sun will also scald and burn the leaves.

WATER: Take care when watering this plant as it is very susceptible to overwatering and root rot. Mist any aerial roots daily to prevent them from drying out, and the compost should be left to dry out before re-watering. When watering, make sure the compost is wet and not soaked. The cup of the plant should always have 1/2-3/4cm (1-2in) of water in to help keep the surrounding humidity high. Change this water once every few days to stop it from going stagnant.

PROPAGATION: The Scarlet Star will occasionally produce offshoot pups from its base, which usually occur after the flowering period. Leave the pups until they are a few centimetres in size and then they can be broken off and repotted.

Its variegated green leaves with bright red veins makes the *Maranta* one of the more attractive house plants to choose. However, the decoration of the leaves is not the only notable feature. It is also known as the Prayer Plant as its leaves are susceptible to night and day; you will notice the leaves raise at the start of the day and then fold and bow down like hands in prayer at night.

A low-growing, creeping plant, it will be happy in a well-drained raised pot or hanging basket, allowing the leaves to flow freely.

HERRINGBONE PLANT
MARANTA LEUCONEURA 'ERYTHRONEURA'

LIGHT: The bright red shades of the Herringbone Plant can fade if they are left in direct sunlight, so place this plant in shady, indirect sunlight during the summer and move to a sunnier spot in the cooler winter months.

WATER: Water your Herringbone Plant once a week and make sure the compost is damp at all times, but do not overwater. Through the winter months you should keep watering to a minimum. Mist regularly to prevent the tips of the leaves going brown and crispy, or even dropping off.

TEMPERATURE: It is important to keep your Herringbone Plant out of any cold draughts. They appreciate an average warmth and any sudden changes can be harmful. Maintain a minimum temperature of 10°C (50°F).

This has perhaps one of the more striking leaf patterns you will see - the large heart-shaped pads are a velvet green with almost luminous white detailing. As the plant shoots out a long stem called a spathe from its base, you will notice how much energy it seems to take the *Anthurium crystallinum* to push out the bizarre long yellow flower or spadix, which actually seems not worth the effort! As it enjoys a high humidity, it is often suggested that you grow Crystal Anthurium in a greenhouse, but with some careful attention you should be able to achieve a prize specimen in your home as well.

CRYSTAL ANTHURIUM
ANTHURIUM CRYSTALLINUM

LIGHT:

Throughout the winter months it is a good idea to give your plant as much light as possible, but keep it out of direct sun in the summer.

WATER:

Throughout the year give the compost a little water every few days to ensure that it is kept damp at all times. Due to its need for a high humidity it is important that the leaves are regularly misted. During winter when the air is dry from the central heating you may wish to mist every day.

PROPAGATION:

You will be able to split the stems of the plant while repotting. It is best to do this in spring just before peak growing season.

The Asparagus Fern can be found trailing from pots and hanging baskets. Grown for its feathery elegant foliage, this deceptive plant is not actually a fern, but part of the *Liliaceae* family. It is much easier to look after than other ferns and does not need a humid environment, but you should give the branches room to spread out so this plant can reach its full potential.

ASPARAGUS FERN

ASPARAGUS SETACEUS

LIGHT:

The Asparagus Fern is fully adaptable to low light or bright conditions, but keep it away from direct sunlight as this can cause yellowing foliage and leaf drop.

WATER:

Water your plant regularly and do not allow the compost to dry out, as this will cause yellowing on the lower leaves. Misting is not necessary but advised during winter to keep the leaves from dropping.

PROPAGATION:

Occasionally the Asparagus Fern will produce small white flowers and berries, so if you are lucky enough to encounter the fruit, they can be planted in soil to propagate. You can also easily propagate your plant by dividing it when repotting. Just be careful to gently tease the spindly stems apart and plant into new pots.

A plant selected for its highly decorative and unusual leaf shape and pattern, the Rattlesnake Plant is native to the jungles of Brazil and will add a touch of the tropics to any home with its bright-green topside leaves that contrast beautifully with the rich purple undersides. Just remember that this plant needs a rich and humid environment so try and copy this as closely as possible.

RATTLESNAKE PLANT

CALATHEA LANCIFOLIA

LIGHT: Keep your Rattlesnake Plant in a shady spot with indirect sunlight, as too much sunshine can discolour the leaves, turning them brown and crispy. This plant does not like rapid changes of temperature and draughts, so try to keep the environment warm without being dry and do not allow the plant to get cold.

WATER: Your Rattlesnake Plant likes a good humid environment. Through the summer months make sure that the compost is kept damp, and mist frequently. During winter, decrease the watering to once every two weeks as the plant will go into dormancy.

POTTING: Repot your Rattlesnake Plant once a year during spring when the plant has outgrown its pot. The Rattlesnake Plant can also be divided at this time. Just separate the stems into as many individual pots as you like.

It is clear to see why this plant, originating from southern China, is also known as the Pancake Plant. Its easily recognisable round, flat leaves make it a focal point in your home, even though it only grows to about 30cm (12in) high. It will chase the sun, so you may notice the more mature plants will curl their woody stem around to reach as much light as possible.

CHINESE MONEY PLANT

PILEA PEPEROMIOIDES

LIGHT: These beauties are partial to a shady spot and grow well on a windowsill in the winter. Do not place them in direct sunlight as this can damage their leaves. They will also enjoy being outside during the summer as long as the weather is fine. If you move them to a shady spot in winter you may also be lucky enough see the bloom of their small white flowers.

WATER: Relatively easy to care for, *Pilea* is happy in a free-draining soil and enjoys being watered once a week when the soil has completely dried out, possibly more often during the hot summer months.

PROPAGATION: This plant can be completely self-propagating. From a young age the plant will start to produce offshoots or pups at the base of the stem. You can also propagate from a cutting. Long stems can be placed in a cup of water and will quickly form strong roots, which when long enough can be planted into moist compost.

Native to the tropics of Sri Lanka, this plant is fussy about air humidity and temperature, so is not that easy to look after. However, it is clear to see where the appeal of the Croton comes from, as the wonderfully colourful leaves and painterly patterns makes it an eye-catching plant to have among all the green in your collection.

JOSEPH'S COAT (CROTON)

CODIAEUM VARIEGATUM VAR. PICTUM

LIGHT: Bright light is essential for the Croton, but keep it out of direct sunlight as this can scald the leaves. However, if your plant does not have enough light you will notice the leaf patterns and colouring fade.

WATER: Water liberally throughout the summer months and keep the compost damp most of the time. If your plant does not get enough water the lower leaves will go brown and drop off. This plant likes high humidity and warm temperatures so mist frequently in summer, every day if possible, and wash the leaves regularly. Do not allow your Croton to get cold or draughty in winter.

POTTING: Repot your Croton in the spring, but be as careful as you can as too much change will cause the plant to drop its leaves. Keep the same compost and keep in the same spot as before if possible.

Native to the Philippines, the *Alocasia* has become more widely available in recent years, and is a welcome addition to any house plant enthusiast looking for something a bit more unusual to add to their collection. Although many different hybrids can now be found, the most popular is the *Alocasia* sanderiana with its erect stems, dark green glossy leaves and striking pale veins.

ELEPHANT'S EAR ALOCASIA SANDERIANA

LIGHT:

Direct summer sun should be avoided as the leaves can easily burn, so keep this plant in a shaded spot and only increase the hours of sunshine in the winter when light is low.

WATER:

In its natural habitat the *Alocasia* is found in damp, humid environments, so to have the most success with your plant you should try to mimic this as best as possible. Throughout the summer do not allow the soil to dry out and mist the leaves frequently.

PROPAGATION:

The *Alocasia* is grown from a rhizome, which can be easily split in the spring when repotting to separate into many smaller plants. The top of rhizome should be planted above the soil to ensure active growth.

WATCH OUT FOR:

Alocasia are especially toxic so please watch out for pets and small children around these plants.

Known as the Cast Iron Plant due to its hardiness and tolerance of neglect, the *Aspidistra* has been a household foliage favourite since the 1970s. It can withstand extremes of light as well as periods of drought.

CAST IRON PLANT

ASPIDISTRA ELATIOR

LIGHT:

Although it is tolerant of most lighting conditions, try to keep your plant out of indirect sunlight as this can scorch the beautiful ribbed leaves.

WATER:

Water roughly once a week throughout the summer, and once every two weeks during the cooler winter months, do not allow the roots to sit on soggy compost as this can be a cause of root rot. The *Aspidistra* does not crave the humidity of most house plants, but it will appreciate having its leaves wiped once in a while.

REPOTTING:

This plant will grow quite happily in the same pot for 4-5 years without any need for repotting. It is always good to check the *Aspidistra* in the spring for overcrowding. If you find this to be the case, then remove any new shoots. Make sure the roots are still attached and repot them separately into moist compost.

The original Rex Begonia originated from India, but unfortunately this species no longer exists; what we see now in shops are the brightly coloured hybrids that have developed from that first kind. Rex Begonias rarely flower, and if they do the flowers should be removed, as this will allow the plant to focus all of its energy on the development of the attractive curling leaves. The leaves will often look lopsided due to the way they uncurl as they grow from the hairy stems, but the real beauty is in the array of colours, patterns and occasional metallic silver sheen that can be seen on them.

REX BEGONIA BEGONIA REX

LIGHT: The leaves of a *Begonia* like to grow to face the sun so you will need to turn the pot occasionally to ensure you have healthy growth on every side of the plant. Place in a bright spot away from any direct sunlight. During winter ensure that your *Begonia* receives a few hours of morning and evening light if possible.

WATER: Keep the compost moist at all times, allowing the top layer to dry out slightly between waterings throughout the summer months. In winter, water more sparingly. A humid atmosphere for your *Begonia* will be appreciated, so mist the surrounding air, but make sure not to get any water on the leaves.

REPOTTING: You should repot your plant every spring as *Begonias* can increase in size very quickly and become root-bound. If this happens your plant is likely to lose the vibrant colours of its leaves.

Native to Mexico, the Ponytail Palm, which is a member of the Lily family, is straightforward to keep as a house plant. It is an unusual plant to look at, as the arching leaves come from a central bulb which sits just outside of the compost. This swollen bulb acts as a storage vessel for water, which means the occasional drying out of the roots will not do it much harm. As it is quite a slow-growing plant, you may only see these as small specimens, however in time the Ponytail Plant can reach heights of up to 1.9m (6ft) or more!

PONYTAIL PALM

BEAUCARNEA RECURVATA

LIGHT:

Bright but not direct light is advisable for this plant. The glossy, arching leaves will increase in strength the more sun they are provided with.

WATER:

Throughout the summer months water thoroughly, allowing the compost to dry out in between waterings. Reduce this routine during the winter to once every two weeks. As mentioned water is often stored in the bulb of the plant so you should refrain from overwatering. Misting is not needed with the Ponytail Palm.

PROPAGATION:

This is not really advised with the Ponytail Palm as it can only be propagated from offsets, which do not occur regularly.

With its remarkable painterly leaves, the *Fittonia* is well favoured among the smaller trailing house plants. They are, however, not the easiest to keep alive in normal home conditions, as they like constant humidity, so they will be at their best housed in a terrarium or bottle garden.

FITTONIA

FITTONIA ALBIVENIS

LIGHT: Native to the jungles of Peru, the *Fittonia* is found under the canopy of other plants and is used to having dappled light, so keep your *Fittonia* out of direct sunshine and place in a shady spot. Too much sunlight can bleach the leaves and fade their bright pink veins.

WATER: This plant will appreciate regular watering. Keep the compost damp, and misting is a must. You will know when your *Fittonia* has dried out as it will become limp and floppy. This does not mean the end of the plant though. Miraculously within an hour of watering you will see the stem and leaves begin to stand upright again.

PROPAGATION: *Fittonia* stems can be easily rooted using rooting solution or simply by placing them in a shallow glass of water. Within a few weeks you will be able to make out tiny new roots forming. Once the roots have grown long and strong repot your plantlet in moist soil.

A strikingly delicate plant with bright green, papery leaves and long, black, elegant stems, the Maidenhair Fern will need lots of attention and humidity throughout the year. Because of these demands the bathroom is always a great location for a Maidenhair, as the humidity from the shower and bath will be a real help.

MAIDENHAIR FERN

ADIANTUM RADDIANUM

LIGHT:

Too much light will lead to scorching and not enough light can contribute to poor growth and yellowing of the fronds, so a happy middle balance will keep your Maidenhair thriving. Indirect morning or afternoon sun without any draughts is perfect.

WATER:

Be sure to keep the compost damp and the air around the fronds nice and humid through the summer months. Misting is vital, but you will also notice that the leaves shed water without actually becoming wet.

PRUNING:

If you come across shrivelled and brown leaves, all is not lost. Try cutting your Maidenhair right back and within time you should see some new growth.

WATCH OUT FOR:

The Maidenhair Fern's fronds are a good signifier of how your plant is doing. Its tips will turn brown if the air is too dry and your plant is lacking humidity. Pale fronds are a sign of a lack of fertiliser and when scorch marks appear your plant is being exposed to too much sunlight.

Definitely a fun plant to have around the house, the Ornamental or Dwarf Pineapple is easy to grow and will provide a talking point with its funny little pink fruit growing from the crown of the plant. Pineapples are part of the *Bromeliad* family and are one of the few that choose to grow from the ground opposed to hanging from trees and branches of other plants.

ORNAMENTAL PINEAPPLE

ANANAS COMOSUS 'VARIEGATUS'

WATER:

Like all *Bromeliads* your Pineapple Plant will collect water in the rosettes of its leaves, so at home water once a week in summer, but allow the compost to dry out between watering. In winter you can decrease watering to once every few weeks.

LIGHT:

Pineapples like to bask in the sunshine, as this is how their fruit will naturally ripen. Make sure to place it in a bright spot, but out of direct sunlight. Too little light and your plant will not flower or produce fruit.

DID YOU KNOW:

?

This evergreen plant can grow leaves up to 1m (3ft) in length and in the summer it produces cone-like clusters of purple flowers, followed by bright red pineapples up to 30cm (12in) long.

Found in the tropical rainforests of South America, the *Phlebodium aureum* does not look to be your typical fern. With delicate paper-like blue leaves that are deeply cut and divided to give a wavy hair-like quality, this is a very attractive and unusual plant to add to your collection. Unlike most ferns the Bear's Paw is an epiphyte so will need a much looser compost mixture than the usual potting compost; something like an orchid mixture would work well. Be sure there is ample drainage to avoid root rot when watering.

BEAR'S PAW FERN

PHLEBODIUM AUREUM 'MANDAIANUM'

LIGHT:
Like most ferns the Bear's Paw favours low lighting and will not appreciate being placed near any direct sun.

WATER:
As long as you use free-draining compost you should keep the *Phlebodium aureum* well watered. Throughout the summer months do not allow the compost to dry out completely. Rather strangely this fern does not enjoy water being poured directly into its centre heart as this may cause the leaves to drop, so try to instead water from the edges. Regular misting will also be needed to keep the leaves looking happy and retaining their blue hues as well as stopping browning of the leaf edges.

PROPAGATION:
Can be easily propagated by division of the plant at repotting stage. This should be carried out during the spring, just before the main growing season.

With its paper-thin leaves that boast the most bright and beautiful pink, green and white details, this is a small showstopper of a house plant. Originating from Madagascar, the Polka Dot Plant is easy to grow and look after, but it has one drawback and that is its relatively short lifespan. After flowering the plant will either move into dormancy or even completely die back. The flowers are a light lavender and grow from a long offshoot. To prolong the life of your plant, pinch back the flowers, as these plants are mainly grown for their foliage.

POLKA DOT PLANT

HYPOESTES PHYLLOSTACHYA

LIGHT:

Bright light is best for this plant. The more light your *Hypoestes* receives the more deep and vibrant its leaf pattern will become. If you start to see solid green patches appearing on the leaves it is an indication that you should move the plant to a sunnier position.

WATER:

Keep the soil damp throughout the summer months and mist frequently to keep the humidity high. During winter, water much less frequently and after flowering refrain from giving too much water. If the plant slips into dormancy, continue to water as usual as soon as new growth starts to occur.

POTTING:

Repot your plant in the spring or when it has outgrown its pot. If you notice your Polka Dot stops growing then it's probably because it has become root-bound; so repot.

Perhaps one of the most favoured house plants, this is called *Monstera* for a reason. Originating from the Mexican and Colombian forests, the *Monstera* is a born climber, known for its outrageous growing potential, so make sure you have enough room for your plant to thrive. Often seen supported by a trusty moss stick, the *Monstera*, aka Swiss Cheese Plant, will grow aerial roots from its stems that try to latch on to the moss stick both for support and to take up any excess moisture.

SWISS CHEESE PLANT

MONSTERA DELICIOSA

LIGHT:

The Swiss Cheese Plant is very easy to look after and is one of the hardiest house plant giants to take on. Although it will enjoy large amounts of dappled sunlight, make sure the plant is never in direct sunshine, as this can burn the leaves.

WATER:

Watering this plant is relatively straightforward. Water thoroughly once a week during the warmer months, then once every two to three weeks during the cooler winter months, allowing the top 2.5cm (1in) of soil to dry between watering. Due to its tropical heritage this plant will also appreciate regular misting to increase the humidity around its leaves.

PROPAGATION:

One of the easiest plants to propagate: simply slice off a young stem at the base and place in a cup of water to root. When you notice a substantial number of roots at the end of the stem, plant into a sandy soil mixture.

Native to Central and South America, this epiphyteis is usually found growing from trees or latching on to other plants on the forest floor. Flowering only occurs once in the lifespan of this plant, but the flower can last for a few years. Once it starts to die back, the main plant will also perish.

PINK QUILL TILLANDSIA CYANEA

LIGHT:

A bright but indirect light will be sufficient for your plants. They will even do well under artificial fluorescent lamps. Although these plants will take as much light as they can get, it is a good idea to keep them out of direct sunlight as this can burn and damage the leaves and flower and can sometimes cause the flower to wilt prematurely.

WATER:

The best time of day to water your plant is early in the morning. Soak the plant or water thoroughly once a week for the best results, making sure it completely dries out in between waterings, to avoid suffocation and rot. While many varieties are drought tolerant they will slip into dormancy if they are not watered enough and the occasional misting will not be enough.

PROPAGATION:

As the flower comes to the end of its life your plant will start to produce offsets or pups from the base of its leaves. After a few months of growing these can be separated, repotted in seed and cutting compost, and kept warm until the plant has fully established.

A leggy plant with attractive scalloped pancake leaves, this plant is known as Lucky Leaves and has culinary and medicinal qualities. It is native to the tropical climates of South Africa and the South Pacific and in many countries is used to heal skin complaints. Lucky Leaves is an evergreen perennial plant – if it starts to overgrow it can be trimmed back just above the surface of the compost, allowing room for new growth.

LUCKY LEAVES

CENTELLA ASIATICA 'LUCKY LEAVES'

LIGHT: Indirect sunlight and shady conditions will be welcomed by the *Centella*. Keep away from direct sunshine as the leaves can easily burn and wilt.

WATER: Keep the compost damp at all times. Misting is not necessary but do not allow the plant to completely dry out.

PROPAGATION: This plant is easy to propagate when repotting by separating the delicate stems. Be careful when teasing these apart as you do not want to damage the roots. Thoroughly water when the plant has been repotted.

WATCH OUT FOR: This plant has been known to irritate the skin so if you are worried wear gloves when handling or repotting.

There are so many choices to make when it comes to choosing a fern for your home, but one of the most beautiful and most popular is the Boston Fern with its lacy patterned leaves and graceful arching fronds.

BOSTON FERN

NEPHROLEPIS EXALTATA 'BOSTONIENSIS'

LIGHT: Despite popular belief, ferns are not wholly shade lovers. In their natural habitat they are used to the dappled bright sunshine of a tropical climate, so they will appreciate being in good indirect sunlight.

WATER: Keep the compost damp at all times. If it does dry out, the tips of the fronds can turn brown. However, make sure you do not leave your Boston Fern in soggy compost as this can lead to root rot. This plant loves a humid environment so mist regularly.

PROPAGATION: Boston Ferns are very easy to propagate. You can either divide and repot it or sometimes it will produce young plants at the end of its shoots. When these come into contact with compost they will start to root, so can be removed carefully and replanted.

DID YOU KNOW: The name Boston Fern comes from a discovery of this species about 100 years ago in Boston, USA, when it was thought that this type of *Nephrolepis* had actually died out. Ever since then, they have often been seen in bathrooms basking in the humidity.

Growing to heights of up to 2.5m (8ft), this tall, elegant house plant has finger-like glossy leaflets radiating out like umbrella spokes – it is clear how *Schefflera* came to be named Umbrella Plant. You can find two varieties of Umbrella Plant: one with all green leaves and one with variegated patterns. Both can be let to tower from floor to ceiling or trimmed and tamed to stay small as a coffee table plant.

UMBRELLA PLANT

SCHEFFLERA ARBORICOLA

LIGHT:

As it enjoys bright light but not direct sunshine, the more light a *Schefflera* receives the more growth is seen. If there is not enough light then it may become quite 'leggy' and the distance between stems can increase, making the plant look like it is balding.

WATER:

Ample watering will promote a healthy plant, so the compost should be kept moist at all times. This plant, however, can be rather forgiving and if you leave the compost to dry out for a week or two it shouldn't give you too many problems in the long run. In this case it is much better to underwater than overwater as that can lead to root rot and sometimes even death.

PROPAGATION:

This plant is quite tricky to propagate. The best way is to take about 5cm (2in) from the growing tip in spring and place in a growing solution. This may take a few attempts though.

If you are looking for a large statement plant then the Sweetheart Vine could be the one. With its decorative, cut-out, glossy green leaves, this can grow to form a full domed bush suitable for most indoor gardeners, as long as you have the room!

SWEETHEART VINE

PHILODENDRON XANADU

LIGHT:

Your *Philodendron* will enjoy partial to bright shade, so keep out of direct sunlight. Warmth is also key in keeping this plant healthy and happy in order to promote strong growth.

WATER:

Water thoroughly through the warm summer months, keeping the compost damp at all times and misting regularly. In winter, decrease watering to once every week or two weeks but make sure the soil is just moist. Due to the size of the leaves of this plant you will need to wipe them regularly. Even in the cleanest homes it is really easy for dust to build up on the leaves making it hard for the plant to take in surrounding moisture.

PROPAGATION:

Use a stem directly from the base of the plant to propagate your *Philodendron*. Cut the stem and place in rooting solution and plant up, making sure the compost is always kept damp.

A showy plant often sporting an array of waxy red flowers, *Anthurium scherzerianum* has long slender leaves, compared to the heart-shaped leaves of *Anthurium andreanum*. Both are grown for their showy red flowers, but there are a few other differences between the two varieties. The *Anthurium scherzerianum* is much smaller than the *Anthurium andreanum* and has a curly spadix compared to the straight one on the flower of the *Anthurium andreanum*.

FLAMINGO FLOWER

ANTHURIUM SCHERZERIANUM

LIGHT:

All *Anthuriums* need protecting from the bright summer sun, as direct sun can cause the leaves to brown. During winter, place your plant in a bright position as the colour can fade from the flowers if it has too little light.

WATER:

Keep the compost damp at all times in the summer, watering once every few days and ensuring that it does not dry out. Decrease watering during winter to once every week or two, but humidity should always be kept high, so mist frequently.

PROPAGATION:

This plant can be propagated when you are repotting. Simply separate the stems. Carry this out once every two years during spring before the start of the active growing period.

It's native to China, Korea and Japan, and you may only have seen the lovely yellow speckled foliage of the *Aucuba japonica* outside. It is only the variegated ones that are suitable as house plants. The long, thin, leathery leaves have decorative perforated edges, which can grow in height up to 1.6m (5ft) or more, but can be tamed and kept small just by some simple pruning.

SPOTTED LAUREL

AUCUBA JAPONICA 'VARIEGATA'

LIGHT:

Bright light and indirect sunshine will be welcomed in the summer months, but not direct heat from the sun. Throughout winter this plant will appreciate being moved to a sunnier spot to gain as much light as possible.

WATER:

Water regularly through the summer then less frequently as the cold winter months draw in, allowing the compost to dry out in between watering. Mist frequently especially in winter when the surrounding air will have dried out from the central heating.

PROPAGATION

You will be able to propagate from stem cuttings in the spring. Flowering is very rare in the home, but you may see small purple flowers in outside bushes. They form in clusters of 10 to 30 spreading across the whole plant.

Perhaps the most well known in the house plant world, the Spider Plant has been gracing homes and offices for decades, probably because of its versatility and ease to grow and propagate. It rarely suffers from pests and the main problem which faces a Spider Plant are brown tips on the leaves.

SPIDER PLANT CHLOROPHYTUM COMOSUM

LIGHT:

Indirect light is the preference for the Spider Plant. Too much direct sunshine can cause the leaves to go brown at the tips and can also make the plant look straggly. Although it is mainly grown for its foliage, with the right amount of light you may be lucky to see stems shooting out from the centre of the plant from which delicate white flowers will bloom.

WATER:

As it prefers to dry out in between waterings, once a week or once every two weeks will be the perfect amount of water for Spider Plants as long as there is adequate drainage. Misting is not necessarily needed as the Spider Plant can tolerate low humidity, but will be appreciated every now and again.

PROPAGATION:

Propagation is made very easy by the Spider Plant's ability to house Spiderettes on the ends of its flowering stems. These will eventually start to root themselves and at this point you can remove them from the stems and repot.

With its violin-shaped, glassy foliage the Fiddle Leaf Fig has become a popular plant for those seeking a larger specimen for their collection. You will notice some looking quite bushy and others standing tall in a more tree-like formation. The only difference between these two is age: the younger plants tend to have leaves all the way down their stems, whereas the older trees would have been pruned and trained over many years so that that the leaves will only grow at the top of the woody trunk, creating the distinctive shape.

FIDDLE LEAF FIG

FICUS LYRATA

LIGHT: Whatever the age or style of your Fiddle Leaf Fig it will enjoy being placed in bright, indirect sunlight. It is quite hardy so should be able to adapt to most locations as long as it does not come into direct sunlight.

WATER: Water generously throughout the summer months, as your Fiddle Leaf Fig will quickly take up any water left in the compost, but do not overwater as this can cause rapid leaf drop. Dry air around the plant can also cause leaf loss so mist every week or so as well. During winter decrease watering to once every two weeks, allowing the compost to dry out completely between watering.

HUMIDITY: Your Fiddle Leaf Fig will be happy with normal room humidity but during the winter, mist the leaves if artificial heating is used.

Perhaps one of the most diverse of the Ficus family, the Weeping Fig gets its name from the narrow, arrow-like leaves that line the delicate woody stems. This is a great plant for beginners, but remember that with *Ficus benjamina*, much like a larger tree, the leaves will drop in winter, which is normal. There are many different variations of this plant: the variegated with beautiful pale green and white leaves, the *Ficus benjamina* 'Baroque' with twisted and spiralled leaves, and the standard *Ficus benjamina* with its narrow and pointed rich, dark, glossy green leaves.

WEEPING FIG FICUS BENJAMINA

LIGHT:

The Weeping Fig will enjoy basking in a few hours of morning sun, but move it before the sun gets too strong, and keep away from the afternoon sun. It can adapt to most conditions though so if you don't have much light then this will be fine as well.

WATER:

Water moderately through the warmer summer months, making sure to allow the compost to dry out in between waterings as the roots do not like sitting in damp compost. Misting is essential as if it gets too dry the leaves will start to fall.

REPOTTING:

Repot this plant every two years in the spring. You can continue to repot until the plant gets too large to handle! You can also train your plant as a bonsai: although it will take a lot of time to prune and wire, it can be one of the most fulfilling approaches to keeping a Weeping Fig.

An insectivore that resembles some kind of hairy caterpillar more than a house plant, the *Drosera capensis* bears rosettes of leaves covered in sticky red hairs which grip on to flies and insects while secreting a liquid. These are one of the easiest carnivorous plants to grow as they will be happy in pretty much any medium and can tolerate most conditions found in the home. They will also rarely slip into dormancy and will happily grow indoors all year round. Some are actually known as a weed due to their resistance to death!

CAPE SUNDEW DROSERA CAPENSIS

LIGHT:

Thriving in bright light, *Drosera capensis* can also tolerate small amounts of direct sunlight. The more light that the plant receives the brighter the hairs on the leaves will turn, thus attracting more insects for food.

WATER:

Throughout the summer months keep the compost moist at all times by watering from below. Place a dish of water under the pot so that as soon as the compost starts to dry out it can take up some more water from the dish. During winter just water when the compost starts to dry out, once a week or so.

GROWTH AND CARE:

Drosera will produce small, elegant pink flowers, which should be removed as they start to wilt, as they can end up sticking to the leaves of the plant creating a barrier for insects.

Asian Pitcher Plants are happiest in their native tropical environments of Thailand, Malaysia and the Philippines, but they have also adapted to live happily in your home. Often these plants are encouraged to grow inside terrariums due to the high-humidity environment that they crave; however, sometimes these sealed glass vessels pose more problems than solutions. It would be best to hang your Pitcher Plant so the bulbous pitcher cups do not become constrained in growth, or even just pop it on a shelf so that they can happily dangle off.

PITCHER PLANT NEPENTHES

LIGHT:

Placed in a bright and sunny location, most species of Pitcher Plants will thrive with a few hours of direct sunlight each day. This will help to ensure the strong growth of the pitcher cups. The more sun this plant receives the darker its cups will start to turn, but if it is not receiving enough light you will start to notice the colour of the leaves and pitchers fading – an indication that its position should be reconsidered.

WATER:

Keep the compost moist at all times and do not allow the cups to dry out. This may mean you will have to fill each one to about halfway once every few weeks. Mist regularly throughout the year to keep the humidity high in the surrounding environment.

GROWTH AND CARE:

You don't need to hunt down flies, or regularly feed your Pitcher Plant as insects will naturally find their way into the cups of your plant.

Unlike most *Bromeliads* or air plants, the Earth Star is a terrestrial plant growing roots into the soil opposed to other *Bromeliads* that choose to latch on to the stems or bark of other plants and trees. It's given the name Earth Star due to their leaf formation, and most plants will only grow a few centimetres off the floor, fanning their tough leaves that come in an array of shades from bright reds to pink.

EARTH STAR CRYPTANTHUS BIVITTATUS

LIGHT:

Used to growing along the floors of its native South American jungles, the Earth Star enjoys a dappled shade and should be kept well away from sunlight. Cleverly you can measure the sun tolerance of this plant by the colours of its leaves. Too much sun and the leaves will start to bleach and burn, but too little light and the red hues will start to turn green.

WATER:

Earth Star is a humidity-loving plant, so the bathroom is a great place to house your plant, as the steam from the bath and shower will help to keep the humidity around the plant high. If this is not your position of choice, mist regularly or place the pot on a bed of pebbles and water instead. Watering from the base of the pot once a week and once every few weeks in winter will also be sufficient.

PROPAGATION:

Like most *Bromeliads*, this plant will only flower once in its lifetime. After flowering the plant will go on to produce pups or offshoots, which should be left to grow to about half the size of the mother plant.

There are so many beautiful types of *Calathea*, each with their own distinct leaf shape and pattern, but the *Calathea roseopicta* is one of the most popular, due to its tropical-looking leaves with purple undersides. The *Calathea* 'Medallion' like most *Calathea* is quite a fussy plant that will not respond well if it is too hot, too cold, too dry or too wet; with the right care though it can grow into an attractive bushy plant up to 60cm (2ft) in height. This plant has the ability to close itself up at night, lifting its widespread arms upwards and narrowing its diameter.

ZEBRA PLANT CALATHEA ROSEOPICTA

LIGHT:

You will notice very quickly if you are giving your *Calathea* too much sun, as direct sunlight will burn and crisp the edges and make for an unattractive and wilting plant.

WATER:

Keep the compost constantly damp but not soaking, and try not to let the compost dry out fully as this can cause leaf browning and dropping. Do not let it stand in a puddle of water as this can cause root rot. Misting and a high humidity is vital, as *Calathea* are very sensitive to low humidity and will quickly drop their leaves or turn brown. Spray with water regularly, and it's best to keep them on a bed of pebbles and water.

PROPAGATION:

Calathea can be propagated when repotting by separation. This is a delicate process and you should be careful not to tear or damage the roots.

Originating from Japan and known for its abundance of lush foliage, the *Hosta* has usually been seen as an outdoors plant, but more recently we are seeing it pop up a lot more in the home. The appeal is largely in its decorative leaf patterns rather than of an elaborate flower. They are relatively easy to care for, and if you have enough space in your home, you can let them reach their full potential at up to 1.6m (5ft) in diameter. All *Hostas* have a dormant period in the winter so they are best grown as annuals: do not be too dismayed if they do die back after a flourishing summer.

PLANTAIN LILY HOSTA

LIGHT:

All *Hostas* grow well in shade, but this can vary between each variety. Some prefer full shade while others will thrive best in partial shade, so make sure to look this up when you buy your plant.

WATER:

When grown inside in a container, your *Hosta* will require plenty of watering. Their compost should be kept damp at all times, and make sure they are especially well watered on hot days during the summer. It is important to make sure there is ample drainage though as soggy roots will cause root rot.

REPOTTING:

This plant can be divided when repotting. Ensure each part of the plant has some roots and shake off any excess compost and repot. This should only be carried out in late spring to early summer.

This trailing *Ficus* is not the first plant to come to mind when one thinks of a *Ficus*. However, these low-creeping variations are great as trailers or climbers and love to make their way up a damp moss stick. Their stems also like to shoot out aerial roots, which help to cling to such objects or the inside of a terrarium if planted in a bottle garden.

CREEPING FIG FICUS PUMILA

LIGHT:
Your *Ficus pumila* is used to creeping along the ground, so it will appreciate a well-shaded spot in your home. A common problem with this plant is brown, crispy leaves, which can easily happen if it is given too much exposure to the sun.

WATER:
Water regularly, especially through the summer months as your trailing *Ficus* should never be allowed to dry out. Frequent misting is also essential to keep the plant looking happy. During winter you can decrease watering slightly but carry on with misting.

PRUNING:
As your plant grows it can start looking a little wild, so it is good to prune it back every spring to rejuvenate and keep it in good shape. The *Ficus* doesn't mind being root-bound to some degree. However, it does like to spread out it roots, so when you do repot your plant, cut back any roots which are outside the main root section. You don't need to do this if you are increasing the pot size.

There are many variations of *Dieffenbachia* to choose from, some with all green leaves, others with variegated and more decorative leaves, but all can reach up to 1.6m (5ft) or more if cared for well.

DUMB CANE DIEFFENBACHIA

LIGHT:

Give your *Dieffenbachia* indirect sun and partial shade throughout the summer months and introduce more light during winter. If the colouring on the leaves starts to fade then it may mean you have exposed your plant to too much direct sunshine, so move it to a shadier spot.

WATER:

Dry air can be fatal to a *Dieffenbachia* so misting and regular watering is a must. During the summer months do not allow the compost to dry out as this can cause browning or leaf drop. Through the winter, water much more sparingly to avoid root rot.

POTTING:

Dieffenbachia prefers well-draining soil and it's best to repot this plant in the spring before the growing season starts. A large *Dieffenbachia* can grow up to 1-1.5m (4-5ft) tall which can sometimes make them top heavy, so be sure to plant it in a heavy pot to keep it stablised.

WATCH OUT FOR:

Earning its name Dumb Cane from its sap, which can cause a temporary inability to speak if ingested, this plant is also very toxic to pets.

This trailing vine will drape happily over a hanging basket or cling to a moss stick and climb using its aerial roots for support. With big, beautiful heart-shaped leaves, this foliage plant is also known as the Sweetheart Vine as well as Devil's Ivy as it is virtually impossible to kill. There is also a variegated form.

DEVIL'S IVY SCINDAPSUS AUREUS

LIGHT:

Unlike most house plants the variegated Devil's Ivy holds a special trait as its pattern can withstand very low-light conditions, which would usually cause patterns to fade. This hardy plant will still look attractive without too much light. If your plant is all green then low light is also not an issue. The ideal conditions are bright but indirect sunlight. Keep all varieties out of direct sun as this can scorch the leaves.

WATER:

Tolerant of sporadic and infrequent watering, the *Scindapsus* will only need watering once a week during summer, decreased to once every couple of weeks in winter. A humid environment will encourage the aerial roots and help prevent the leaves browning, so mist frequently.

PROPAGATION:

This plant is very easy to propagate. Just carefully cut one of the stems off the main plant and place it in a cup of water to root. Once rooted, plant the stem in some potting compost and watch it grow!

Native to South America this *Peperomia* is grown mainly for its attractive leaves. Pretty slow growing, this bushy plant will eventually reach around 10-15cm (4-6in) in height. The *Peperomia* will produce curious 'rat-tail' stalks from the base, which do not necessarily flower but do add a funny feature to the plant!

WATERMELON BEGONIA

PEPEROMIA ARGYREIA

LIGHT:

In its natural habitat this plant would be found under trees in a bright but shady spot, so it is best to try to replicate this in your home. As it is small you could easily place it under a taller plant to shield it from direct sun, which can scald the leaves and leave permanent damage.

WATER:

Watering needs to be carefully monitored with these plants. To a certain degree the compost should dry out a little between waterings. However, if the roots get too dry then the leaves will start to fall from the plant so finding a happy medium is key. It is a good idea to use tepid water and water much less frequently through the winter months.

PROPAGATION:

Peperomia is particularly easy to propagate, especially from cuttings. Trim the leaf from the bottom of the stem, then either place in a cup of water and wait until it roots, or dip the bottom of the stem in rooting solution and repot straight away.

The highly decorative spotty spear leaves of the *Begonia maculata* make it a winning choice among the foliage *Begonias*. A tall plant with cane-like stems, this *Begonia* may need support from a gardening pole as it grows to protect the stem from any damage and encourage new leaves. This plant will thrive if planted in a terrarium or bottle garden.

SPOTTED BEGONIA

BEGONIA MACULATA

LIGHT:

Keep your *Begonia maculata* in bright, indirect light to encourage strong growth. However, turn the pots occasionally so that the leaves develop in all directions.

WATER:

Keep the compost moist through the summer months, but do not overwater or allow any water to catch on the leaves as this can scar them if they come into contact with bright sunlight. Water much more sparingly in winter. Your *Begonia* thrives in humidity, so mist the surrounding air, but do not allow any water on the leaves.

POTTING:

It is a good idea to repot this plant every spring as leaves of a root-bound plant can lose their colour.

PROPAGATION:

It is easy to propagate through leaf cutting and standing in shallow water until new roots form, then carefully planting in a seed and cutting compost mixture.

This is a complex-looking trailing plant that has long, slender, hair-like runners that can reach up to 1m (3ft) long and house miniature plants on the ends. Ideally, plant it in a hanging pot to give it enough space so that the runners don't get too tangled. Throughout the summer months you may also see some small, insignificant flowers gathering; however, these plants are grown mainly for their olive-green leaf pattern and their strange growing habits rather than their flowers.

MOTHER-OF-THOUSANDS

SAXIFRAGA SARMENTOSA

LIGHT:

Keep away from direct sunshine, although the *Saxifraga* will thrive in a brightly lit spot, which will encourage summer flowering.

WATER:

During the summer growing period, water your plant freely and do not allow the compost to dry out. In winter, keep watering to a minimum as the *Saxifraga* is especially susceptible to root rot. Occasional misting will also be welcomed.

PROPAGATION:

This is a very easy plant to propagate. Take one of the young plantlets and pin it down in a small pot of compost until it roots, then you can cut off the stem and plant.

With a tall, thin trunk that branches with age, the *Dracaena marginata* is a favourite among house plants. It is also known as a false palm because of its top crown of long, thin leaves. This plant is tolerant to neglect, which is why you may regularly see it in the corners of offices and doctors' waiting rooms; but be assured only the best care will ensure that it reaches its full potential growing height of up to 3m (10ft) tall.

FLAMING DRAGON TREE

DRACAENA MARGINATA

LIGHT:

A slightly shady spot with regular intervals of indirect sunlight is the perfect environment for your Flaming Dragon Tree. It is relatively hardy so it can tolerate low light, but if it has long periods of low light then it can become leggy and the leaves quite spindly.

WATER:

Keep the compost moist at all times and do not allow it to dry out completely, especially during summer, as this can cause the leaves to turn brown and dry. You can decrease watering in winter to once every few weeks and only water once the compost starts to dry out.

DID YOU KNOW:

?

The Flaming Dragon tree is an air-filtering plant and is part of Nasa's Clean Air Study. This plant naturally reduces benzene, formaldehyde, xylene and toluene in the air. But keep away from cats and dogs as it can be poisonous to pets.

The ever-popular Peace Lily is a firm favourite due to its delicate, arum-like white flower which can appear in spring, and if you are lucky, again in the autumn. It sits up there with some of the best house plants for air purification, so is a great choice if you are considering one for the living room or bedroom.

PEACE LILY SPATHIPHYLLUM WALLISII PEACE LILY

LIGHT:

Your Peace Lily will thrive in indirect sunlight, and will appreciate being kept out of any intense sunshine. It enjoys being kept warm, especially in winter, so keep away from any cool draughts. The brighter and warmer your home the more flowers you should expect to see each year. Low light will make it appear more of a green foliage plant.

WATER:

The long, glossy leaves are very receptive to water and will wilt quickly if the compost is too dry, so try to keep the compost moist at all times without overwatering. The leaves will appreciate a wiping and dusting to keep them looking fresh. Mist regularly to keep the humidity high around the plant.

PROPAGATION:

The stems can be divided during repotting to propagate. This should be carried out each year in the spring when the plant is about to move into its growing season.

This sweet little plant has one special feature: as soon as its delicate leaves are touched during the day they rapidly fold up and the stems start to droop, taking about an hour to recover! This will, however, also happen naturally in the evening. An easy plant to look after, the *Mimosa pudica* will also produce the most beautiful fluffy pink ball flowers through the summer months.

SENSITIVE PLANT MIMOSA PUDICA

LIGHT:

Although known as the Sensitive Plant due to its responsive leaves, this should not be taken into account when it comes to how much light to give it. Your plant will thrive in bright light and can also take small amounts of direct sunlight.

WATER:

The compost should ideally be kept damp through the summer months, without overwatering. During winter keep watering to a minimum and allow the compost to slightly dry out between waterings.

HUMIDITY:

The *Mimosa* enjoys a high humidity so regular misting of the leaves is advised, especially during winter when the central heating can really dry them out.

PRUNING:

Prune your *Mimosa* regularly to keep it full and prevent it from becoming leggy.

This plant is known as the Arrowhead or Goose Foot Plant due to its heart-shaped leaves of the younger plant. An unusual feature is the dramatic change in leaf shape as the plant matures. Morphing from a singular point in the leaf on an erect stalk into well-lobed leaves with stems that have a tendency to climb and produce aerial roots, which will cling to moss sticks or supports. This is an attractive foliage plant that will do well if placed in a tall pot when young, it can then be transferred to a hanging pot when the stems start to climb.

ARROWHEAD PLANT

SYNGONIUM PODOPHYLLUM

LIGHT: For variegated types bright but indirect light is ideal. Keep away from any strong sun as this can scorch and damage the delicate leaves. If you have an all-green specimen then a more shaded spot is preferred. You may have to turn the plant occasionally so that all sides get the same amount of light and to prevent an uneven growing pattern.

WATER: Keep the compost moist at all times and do not allow it to dry out as the plant is very susceptible to wilting quickly. Decrease the watering in winter when it goes into dormancy. A humid environment is required so mist the leaves every few days.

PROPAGATION: This plant is very easy to propagate using the stems that already bear the aerial roots.

The beauty in these plants is in the metallic silver and purple coating that each leaf boasts. Their striking patterns shimmer in the sun and they are grown mainly for the trailing potential of the foliage. The Inch Plant is known to grow at rapid rates, hence its name. It will do very well in a hanging basket and can be trained to grow up or down a moss pole. Because of its fast-growing pace, the Inch Plant does not do too well with age - the longer its legs get the more leaves seem to be lost near the base of the plant. No matter how keen you are to pinch back the vines this legginess is pretty much unavoidable.

INCH PLANT TRADESCANTIA ZEBRINA

LIGHT:

The Inch Plant appreciates bright sunlight, so this is essential and even some direct sun will be beneficial to the growth and strength of its leaves. If not enough light is given to this plant you may notice the colour fading from the leaves as well as bare and spindly growth on the stems.

WATER:

From spring to autumn water this plant liberally, allowing the compost to dry out between watering. Throughout winter ensure watering is decreased to once every few weeks. Misting will be appreciated, but is not necessary.

PROPAGATION:

The Inch Plant will root very easily. Take stem cuttings in spring to autumn and place in damp compost without the use of rooting solutions.

Native to the southern islands of Japan, the *Fatsia japonica* is suited to hot and humid summers followed by cooler and drier winter months. However, it is susceptible to very cold and dry conditions, so should be kept away from draughts or wind. It has large, deeply cut leaves that feel as fragile as thin paper, so you can see where this plant gets its name from. The leaves can sometimes grow up to 30cm (1ft) in width and the stems grow out in various directions, so give this plant plenty of room to grow.

PAPER PLANT FATSIA JAPONICA

LIGHT:

Your *Fatsia* will grow best in partial to full shade. Small amounts of sun will be beneficial in the morning and afternoon, but too much will bleach out the dark green leaves, turning them yellow and dull.

WATER:

Water regularly but do not allow the soil to dry out completely during the summer growing season. Mist regularly to keep the surrounding environment humid. Hold back from watering as frequently through the winter months and ensure that the roots do not sit in water as this plant is particularly susceptible to root rot.

PRUNING:

To ensure a healthy and bushy show, prune this plant at the start of each growing season in early spring, otherwise it will start to get quite long and leggy and will not look as attractive.

This may be one of the most resilient and hardy house plants you can find - when looking at a Zanzibar Gem one could actually mistake it for a plastic plant. It is made up of individual stems which can each grow up to 1.6m (5ft) in height, and each is lined with glossy, rubber-like leaves. This house plant can tolerate the highest and lowest of light conditions as well as doing very well in drought, if you are not regular at watering your plants! However, like most plants it does have its preferences.

ZANZIBAR GEM

ZAMIOCULCAS ZAMIIFOLIA

LIGHT: As mentioned this plant will do well in low lighting but to maximise growth and the glossy leaves, it would be ideal to place it in a bright location, avoiding direct sun.

WATER: It is better to underwater than overwater your Zanzibar Gem. Water once a week in the summer months, allowing the top layer of compost to dry out in between watering. Water more sparingly during winter and do not worry too much about misting as it is not too fussed about a humid environment.

PROPAGATION: This plant is very easy to propagate as it is made up of rhizomes which can be separated at the root when repotting. It does not mind being root-bound so the likelihood of you needing to repot more than every few years is low.

A firm favourite since the Victorian times, the Bamboo Palm is exceptionally easy to care for and will tolerate almost any environment. You will often see these palms in a range of different sizes – they work well as a small table-top specimen, but if cared for well they can reach heights of up to 80cm (32in).

BAMBOO PALM

CHAMAEDOREA SEIFRIZII

LIGHT:

Preferring a bright spot with indirect sunshine, the Bamboo Palm will also do well in low light conditions, which makes it a versatile plant perfect for any environment. Just be sure to keep it out of direct sunlight as it will scorch the leaves and turn them brown. As with most house plants though, the more sun your plant receives the more you should expect the plant to grow.

HUMIDITY:

It enjoys a humid environment, so mist your palm regularly. When watering ensure the compost is kept damp at all times, but without being drenched through. During the summer months your palm should be watered once a week, then throughout winter decrease the watering to once every few weeks.

DID YOU KNOW:

?

They are also well known for their air-purification capabilities and are a solid choice if you are considering a plant for its stature and health benefits. Look for dark green and strong leaves when selecting a palm.

The *Yucca* is naturally found in South America so can handle most conditions. This woody and dominating house plant with its spiky, strong leaves make it a sturdy choice and can add structure to any house plant collection.

YUCCA YUCCA ELEPHANTIPES

LIGHT:

Provide your *Yucca* with as much light as possible. It can cope with small amounts of direct light during winter as this will help to encourage strong leaves, but keep it out of indirect sun during the warm summer months. Low light can result in droopy or saggy leaves, so if this happens move the plant to a brighter and sunnier spot.

WATER:

Water quite liberally from spring to autumn, but make sure your *Yucca* is planted in free-draining compost as it is susceptible to root rot. Decrease winter watering to a couple of times a month and only water when the compost has completely dried out. Misting is not necessary.

PROPAGATION:

The *Yucca* will often sprout small offsets at the base of its stem, which can be taken out and repotted.

REPOTTING:

Repot your *Yucca* every two years in spring. It has a tendency to become top heavy so planting it in a deep container will help prevent it from toppling over.

One of the most recognisable foliage plants, Ivy is usually found growing outside, but as long as you know what makes this trailing plant happy it will grow well in your home, too. Ivy is a climbing plant so it is best to use a hanging basket or moss stick to train the stems, and watch out for the aerial roots, as Ivy tends to try and cling to any surface around it.

IVY HEDERA HELIX

LIGHT: The most important factor to consider when growing Ivy indoors is light. All Ivy requires lots of light: the brighter the better. Variegated cultivars will require less light but be aware that the less light it gets the less pronounced the variegated pattern will be. Lack of light will also cause your plant to become 'leggy' and maybe more prone to pests.

WATER: Keep the soil on the dry side when watering your Ivy as it does not like to be left standing in water and must have adequate drainage. Throughout the summer months water your Ivy once a week when the compost is dry to the touch. During winter, decrease the watering to once every two weeks or again wait until the soil has dried out.

GROWTH AND CARE: Help your Ivy thrive indoors by misting its leaves regularly and protecting it from cold draughts and heating vents. Misting will help keep spider mites at bay and wash the leaves will get rid of any dust or pests.

Native to Australia, the *Platycerium bifurcatum* is one of the few ferns that do not exhibit a coiled crozier as it grows. The large antler-like fronds are divided at the ends, which gives this fern its name of Staghorn. A showy foliage plant that is easy to look after in the home, this plant is made up of two types of fronds: the sterile kidney-shaped fronds at the base of the plant and the divided spore-bearing fertile ones above.

STAGHORN FERN

PLATYCERIUM BIFURCATUM

LIGHT:

Staghorn Ferns will grow best in bright, indirect sunshine, as they will burn in direct sun.

WATER:

If your fern is mounted on a wall, you should water thoroughly without allowing any water to get caught between the fronds. Pools of water will quickly rot your Staghorn. Planted-up Staghorn Ferns should be watered from below. Fill up the tray your pot stands in and allow it to take up as much water as needed within about a 15-minute time scale. If you repeat once a week through the summer months and less frequently throughout winter this will be enough without soaking the roots of the plant. As it is used to the high humidity of rainforests, regularly mist your Staghorn Fern throughout the year.

PROPAGATION:

Staghorn Ferns will create a large amount of offsets or pups, which can be easily removed and replaited or remounted on a wall.

Despite its name the Ti Plant is not actually native to Hawaii – its decorative red leaves would usually be seen in Southeast Asia, but the people of Hawaii have found many uses for it such as their famous grass skirts and surfboard covers! Also known as the False Palm because of the spray of strong, sword-like leaves, there are three main types of *Cordyline*, but the red-edged Ti Plant is the most popular choice for a house plant. You may notice in older plants the lower leaves of the *Cordyline* dying off. This will just promote new growth at the top of the plant so remove these leaves and discard.

HAWAIIAN TI PLANT

CORDYLINE TERMINALIS

LIGHT: The brightest spot you can find, without being in any direct sun, will be ideal for your Ti Plant. With too little light the growth will be stunted and you may notice curling leaves, but if the leaves are exposed to direct sunlight they will start to scorch and bleach.

WATER: Ensure you have a free-draining pot and water regularly throughout the summer months; allowing the top of the soil to dry out in between watering. During winter, water much more sparingly.

HUMIDITY: Your *Cordyline* will appreciate a humid environment so mist around the leaves frequently. If the tips of the leaves start to brown and yellow you may need to place the pot on a tray of wet pebbles to increase the humidity in the surrounding area.

An epiphytic, used to trailing off the trees in the jungles of Southeast Asia, the *Aeschynanthus lobbianus* can span up to 60cm (2ft) in length and will provide an unusual hanging plant in your home. For best results, pot in a hanging basket to allow the thick, rubbery leaves and delicate flowers hang freely, without being knocked. Quite often you will be able to purchase the Lipstick Plant when it is flowering, but in reality it is quite tricky to get these plants to flower every year. The best thing to do is to cut back the stems once the flowering season is over and this will entice more flowers the following year.

LIPSTICK PLANT

AESCHYNANTHUS LOBBIANUS

LIGHT: During the summer months keep your Lipstick Plant in a bright spot away from any direct sunlight. This can be altered in winter when a few hours of direct sun is beneficial. Bright sun will encourage flowering during spring and summer.

WATER: It is best to use tepid water for your Lipstick Plant. Water thoroughly throughout spring and summer, allowing the compost to dry between waterings. Decrease watering during winter when the plant goes into dormancy. Water just enough so that the leaves do not start to crumple.

HUMIDITY: This plant enjoys a high humidity, so mist the leaves regularly or place near a tray of water and pebbles to increase the humidity around the plant as the water evaporates.

This beautiful indoor tree is the best way to get some new structure and height into your house plant collection. It is pretty much indestructible and can be as large or as small as you wish. Originating from the swamps of South America, this plant can stand excessively damp soil and excessively bright sun! Young *Pachira* have their trunks braided to create the unusual plaited pattern you will see on most of the plants available to buy, so as they grow in your home, the plait will continue as well.

GUIANA CHESTNUT PACHIRA AQUATICA

LIGHT:

Indirect sun is most favoured by the *Pachira*. If the leaves start to yellow this indicates the need for more light. Try to move it to a sunnier location but still away from any strong, direct sun.

WATER:

As the *Pachira* is used to the swampy surroundings of the South American wetlands, it can tolerate a heavy amount of watering as long as there is a good drainage. You still will not want the roots sitting in a tray of water and you should allow the top few centimetres to dry out in between watering. As the growth slows down in the winter, decrease the watering, but mist both the trunk and leaves throughout the year.

PRUNING:

You can grow your *Pachira* as a bonsai. Grow it in a small container to control its size, regularly pruning and pinching off tips.

The words Bonsai literally means 'planted in a pot'. The art of growing these dwarfed trees in shallow containers dates back to the twelfth century in China. It was picked up by the Japanese who then perfected the art. Quite a few Bonsai are deciduous. This means that they will lose their leaves through the winter months just like the larger outdoor versions. If yours starts to do this it is a good idea to check the species to determine if this is normal for your plant.

BONSAI

WATER:

One of the main things to remember about most Bonsai is that they will only thrive if the soil is kept damp. In fact, this is very important in keeping the plant alive. Even if you forget to water for a few days the plant may die. Most Bonsai will also appreciate a high humidity so mist the leaves every few days.

LIGHT:

A surprising fact about many Bonsai is that they crave direct sunlight. For most plants this would be detrimental, but as long as the room is airy and not too stuffy the general rule is the more light the better! If there is little airflow is can cause the tree to dry out too quickly and potentially lead to a fatality.

PRUNING:

Pruning and repotting is essential for a Bonsai. You will need to prune new growth regularly in order to keep its form and shape. You will notice larger leaves shooting out of some stems, so trim these back to keep only the smaller ones. Repotting will be necessary once every two to three years when the tree has become root-bound or the roots start to outgrow the pot. Make sure to only repot during spring just before the most active growing period.

PEPPER TREE BONSAI

The Pepper Tree Bonsai on p134 has been trained and planted into a miniature forest. This is a common technique used to display multiple trees in one tray. The Pepper Tree itself is a rather unusual plant as it is the actual species used to produce Szechuan peppercorns! It is relatively easy to keep and maintain for beginners, and the tiny leaves are a rich and glossy green in summer, occasionally producing small red flowers. They turn golden and orange in autumn, then finally drop off in winter. It is a rather thirsty Bonsai, so you must keep the soil damp at all times without being soaked, and mist frequently to ensure it does not dry out. Yearly root trimming may be necessary as the root growth on these trees is rapid.

ULMUS PARVIFOLIA 'CHINESE ELM'

A popular Bonsai that can be grown both inside and out, the Chinese Elm is a medium-sized tree that can be easily trained to shape and curve the trunk. As soon as the soil gets dry these Elms should be watered. They will suffer without enough water and will start to die and lose their leaves. If left outside in winter the tree will inevitably drop its leaves, but if you keep it inside and away from any central heating the branches should retain most of their leaves year round.

PEPPER TREE BONSAI

ULMUS PARVIFOLIA 'CHINESE ELM'

One of the house plants that likes to take on a false identity, this *Cycad* is palm-like in appearance, but is not related to the true palms, such as the Kentia or Reed Palms. As it is an extremely slow-growing plant you will need to invest time to enjoy its one-leaf-per-year development. However it's worth the wait as after a while you will be witness to the symmetry of a dark green rosette of spiky, arching leaves.

JAPANESE SAGO PALM

CYCAS REVOLUTA

LIGHT:

Cycads prefer a bright, sunny spot, which will encourage strong and stable root growth. They will also tolerate a low light.

WATER:

This palm will not respond well to too much water, so water once a week. Make sure it is planted in free-draining compost and allow it to to dry out fully between watering. *Cycads* do not require a high humidity, so misting is not necessary.

PROPAGATION:

Seeds from this palm can take months to germinate and years to grow into a tree. Mature plants will grow offsets called pups which can be separated and planted into their own pots.

WATCH OUT FOR:

This palm is poisonous to pets so avoid if you have a cat or dog.

INDEX

A
Adiantum raddianum
52-3
Aeschynanthus
lobbianus 128-9
Alocasia 'Dragon
Scale' 24-5
A. sanderiana 42-3
Ananas comosus
'variegatus' 54-5
Anthurium crystallinum
32-3
A. scherzerianum
72-3
Arrowhead Plant 110-11
Asparagus Fern 13,
34-5
Asparagus setaceus 13,
34-5
Aspidistra elatior 44-5
Aucuba japonica
'Variegata' 74-5

B
Bamboo Palm 118-19
Banana Plant 20-1
Bear's Paw Fern 56-7
Beaucarnea recurvata
48-9
Begonia 9
B. maculata 100-1

B. rex 46-7
Bonsai 132-3
Pepper Tree Bonsai
133, 134
Ulmus parvifolia
'Chinese Elm' 133, 135
Boston Fern 66-7
burning 14
buying plants 9

C
Calathea 9
C. lancifolia 13, 36-7
C. roseopicta 88-9
Cape Sundew 82-3
Cast Iron Plant 44-5
Centella asiatica 'Lucky
Leaves' 64-5
Chamaedorea seifrizii
118-19
Chinese Money Plant
38-9
Chlorophytum
comosum 12, 76-7
Codiaeum variegatum
var. pictum 40-1
compost 10
containers 10
Cordyline terminalis
126-7
Creeping Fig 92-3

Croton 40-1
Cryptanthus bivittatus
86-7
Crystal Anthurium 32-3
cuttings 12
Cycas revoluta 136-7

D
Devil's Ivy 96-7
Dieffenbachia 94-5
diseases 9
Dracaena marginata
104-5
Dragon Scale 42-3
Drosera capensis 82-3
Dumb Cane 94-5

E
Earth Star 86-7
Elephant's Ear 24-5

F
False Palm 126-7
False Shamrock 18-19
Fatsia japonica 9,
114-15
ferns 9
Bear's Paw Fern 56-7
Staghorn fern 124-5
Ficus benjamina 80-1
F. elastica 26-7

F. lyrata 78-9
F. pumila 92-3
Fiddle Leaf Fig 78-9
figs
    Creeping Fig 92-3
    Fiddle Leaf Fig 78-9
    Weeping Fig 80-1
Fittonia albivenis 50-1
Flaming Dragon Tree
    104-5
Flamingo Flower 72-3
fungus gnat 14

G
Goose Foot Plant
    110-11
growth, poor 15
Guiana Shestnut 130-1
Guzmania lingulata
    28-9

H
hanging plants 9
Hares Foot 56-7
Hawaiian Ti Plant
    126-7
Hedera helix 122-3
Herringbone Plant
    30-1
Hosta 90-1
humidity, adding 11
Hypoestes
    phyllostachya 58-9

I
Inch Plant 112-13
Ivy 122-3

J
Japanese Sago Palm
    136-7
Joseph's Coat 40-1

L
leaves
    cuttings 12
    shedding 15
    yellowing 14
Lipstick Plant 128-9
Lucky Leaves 64-5

M
Maidenhair Fern 52-3
Maranta leuconeura
    'Erythroneura' 30-1
mealy bugs 15
Mimosa pudica 108-9
misting 9, 11
Monstera 9
    M. deliciosa 60-1
    M. obliqua 22-3
Mother-of-Thousands
    102-3
Musa oriana 20-1

N
Nepenthes 84-5

Nephrolepis exaltata
    'Bostoniensis' 66-7

O
offshoots (pups) 12
Ornamental Pineapple
    54-5
overwatering 14
Oxalis triangularis
    18-19

P
Pachira aquatica 130-1
Pancake Plant 38-9
Paper Plant 9, 114-15
Parlour Palm 118-19
Peace Lily 106-7
pebble tray 11
Peperomia argyreia
    98-9
Pepper Tree Bonsai
    133-4
pests 9, 14-15
Philodendron xanadu
    70-1
Phlebodium aureum
    'Mandaianum' 56-7
Pilea 12
    P. peperomiodes
    38-9
Pineapple, Ornamental
    54-5
Pink Quill 62-3

Pitcher Plant 84-5
Plantain Lily 90-1
plants
  choosing 9
  propagating 12-13
Platycerium bifurcatum
  124-5
Polka Dot Plant 58-9
Ponytail Palm 48-9
pots 10
Prayer Plant 30-1
propagation 12-13
pups (offshoots) 12

R
Rattlesnake Plant 13,
  36-7
Rex Begonia 46-7
root rot 14
Rubber Plant 26-7

S
Saxifraga 12
  S. sarmentosa 102-3
Scarlet Star 28-9
Schefflera arboriciola
  68-9
sciarid fly 14
Scindapsus aureus
  96-7
scorching 14
Sensitive Plant 108-9
separating plants 12

shedding 15
snips 10
Spathiphyllum wallisii
  106-7
spider mites 15
Spider Plant 12, 76-7
Spotted Begonia 100-1
Spotted Laurel 74-5
Staghorn fern 124-5
stem cuttings 12
Sweetheart Vine 70-1,
  96-7
Swiss Cheese Plant
  60-1
Swiss Cheese Vine
  22-3
*Syngonium
  podophyllum* 110-11

T
Ti Plant, Hawaiian
  126-7
Tillandsia cyanea 62-3
tools 10
Tradescantia zebrina
  112-13
trailing plants 9
troubleshooting 14-15

U
Ulmus parvifolia
  'Chinese elm' 133, 135
Umbrella Plant 68-9

W
watering 10
  overwatering 14
Watermelon Begonia
  98-9
Weeping Fig 80-1
wilting 14

Y
yellowing leaves 14
Yucca elephantipes
  120-1

Z
Zamioculcas zamiifolia
  116-17
Zanzibar Gem 116-17
Zebra Plant 88-9

Aerial root: A root that grows out from the stem above ground level. Aerial roots are commonly found on Swiss Cheese Plants.

Bonsai: The art of dwarfing trees by careful root and stem pruning.

Crozier: The curled top of a young fern.

Frond: A leaf of a fern or palm.

Hardy: A plant that can withstand adverse growing conditions, tolerating cold, heat, drought, flooding or draughts.

Humidity: A measure of the amount of water vapour in the air. Plants that originated from a jungle environment like to live in a humid atmosphere, which should be replicated in the home with a water mister.

Leaf node: A small swelling that occurs on a plant stem from which one or more leaves emerge.

Leggy: A plant that has long, spindly, often leafless stems. When this occurs you may find your plant produces fewer flowers and becomes prone to flopping over. To combat this make sure your plant gets adequate light, and prune it back to encourage thicker growth.

Offset: A young plantlet that appears on a mature plant. These can usually be carefully detached and used for propagation.

Plantlets: Young or small plants that grows off of a parent plant, which can be propagated.

Pup: A plant that develops as an offset from a parent plant.

Root-bound: The roots of a plant that has outgrown its pot and will grow in circles, becoming cramped and tangled.

Spathe: A large bract, enclosing the flower cluster of certain plants, especially the spadix of arums and palms.

SUPPLIERS

The publisher wishes to thank the following suppliers for their generous loans of pots and ceramics for the book.

CONPOT
A glorious collection of concrete planters in a range of sizes.
fromtheland.studio

ELLA HOOKWAY
A beautiful range of clean, functional forms made using monochromatic slabs of procelain and stoneware clay.
ellahookway.com

LAZY GLAZE – HARRIET LEVY-COOPER
Ceramics that showcase the intrinsic qualities of the clay's natural tones and textures.
lazyglaze.co.uk

LOUISE MADZIA
A chic collection of planters with quirky illustrations.
louisemadzia.com

MAE CERAMICS
A gorgeous selection of minimalist ceramics with a playful glaze.
maeceramics.com

MIA MARGETIC
A creative range of cute but simple ceramic planters.
miamargetic.com

MILO MADE
Industrial ceramics with a pop of colour.
milomade.net

PAPERCHASE
A shop that fulfills all your paper, cards and craft needs.
www.paperchase.co.uk

POT PARTY
Fun collection of delightful planters.
potparty.co.uk

REPEAT CLAY
A colourful collections of pots.
repeatrepeatrepeatclay.com

SMUG
Independent homewares shop that celebrates great design.
ifeelsmug.com

WEST ELM
Modern furniture and home decor.
westelm.co.uk

ABOUT THE AUTHOR

Emma Sibley has had a keen interest in horticulture from a young age, and after studying Surface Design at university she changed career direction to work with plants. She took a number of courses to increase her knowledge and love of all things green. Emma founded London Terrariums - a shop and business that offers workshops, interior displays and private commissions. She is a member of the British Cactus and Succulent Society.

ACKNOWLEDGEMENTS

I would like to thank all of the amazing ceramists that loaned their beautiful pots and planters for the shoot.

www.londonterrariums.com
106a New Cross Road
London SE14 5BA

PUBLISHING DIRECTOR Sarah Lavelle
EDITOR Harriet Butt
DESIGN AND ART DIRECTION Gemma Hayden
PHOTOGRAPHER Adam Laycock
PROPS STYLIST Rachel Vere
PRODUCTION DIRECTOR Vincent Smith
PRODUCTION CONTROLLER Jessica Otway

Published in 2018 by Quadrille,
an imprint of Hardie Grant Publishing

Quadrille
52–54 Southwark Street
London SE1 1UN
quadrille.com

Reprinted in 2018 (four times), 2019 (five times)
15 14 13 12 11 10

Cataloguing in Publication Data: a catalogue record
for this book is available from the British Library.

Text © Emma Sibley 2018
Design, layout and photography © Quadrille 2018

ISBN 978 1 78713 171 2

Printed in China